GUARDING THE JUICE

How O.J. Simpson Became My Prison BFF

ISBN-13: 978-0-9972920-0-8
ISBN-10: 0-9972920-0-8

First printing: March 2016

Front cover artwork by Deborah Cidboy
 (www.debsrealm.com)

Additional illustrations by Jesse Miller

Cover design by ThomasMax

Published by:

tm

ThomasMax Publishing
P.O. Box 250054
Atlanta, GA 30325
www.thomasmax.com

GUARDING THE JUICE

How O.J. Simpson Became My Prison BFF

By JEFFREY FELIX
With Corey Levitan

ThomasMax

Your Publisher
For The 21st Century

INTRODUCTION

I was offered a sizable bribe not to publish this book. By O.J. Simpson. So say my former co-workers at Lovelock Correctional Center, where I was a prison guard for 20 years.

"I just wish Felix would shut up already," he told one of them. "I'd pay him a million dollars to shut up."

But O.J. Simpson doesn't have that kind of money anymore. He earns $150 a week from an NFL pension and that's it.

This is not an O.J. book. I'm telling you now, while you can still return it as new. I'm sure it contains insight into the way his mind works, and fills in some gaps in the woefully inaccurate historical record amassed by the tabloids. But to me, it's the story of a personal experience that I'm still sometimes not even sure was real.

I was O.J.'s most trusted confidante during the first seven years of his only prison stay. He called me his "best friend after A.C.," referring to Al Cowlings, his chauffeur during the infamous Bronco chase.

That's not an honor that struck me as particularly honorable. You see, I know that O.J. Simpson killed his ex-wife, Nicole Brown Simpson, and waiter Ronald Goldman on the night of June 12, 1994. Not because he admitted it to me (I don't think he's admitted it to anyone – including himself.) I know because, despite how badly the LAPD effed up, the evidence was overwhelming. Even O.J.'s attorney and former best friend Robert Kardashian admitted the following during a 1996 Barbara Walters interview: "The blood evidence is the biggest thorn in my side. That causes me the greatest problems. So I struggle with the blood evidence."

But I also know for a personal reason. When you get to know someone extremely well, you know when that person is lying, or being deceptive. The eyes either refuse to look into yours or focus a little too intensely, as though being forced. Or maybe it's not even that. You just *know*.

There is nothing special about my life, and that's always been perfectly OK with me. At every turn, I made decisions ensuring this fact. I opted for a secure but boring career, in a remote place, requiring the least amount of education and doing the least amount of work possible.

The universe had other plans for me. Imagine falling asleep while watching *A Nightmare on Elm Street*. Then you wake up and everything in the universe is exactly the same except that Freddy Krueger is now real. Oh, and by the way, you hang out with him every day and he's one of the coolest, most well-behaved, respectful people you've ever met. *That's* how it felt.

There's a Safeway supermarket seven miles from the Lovelock prison. Twice a week for most of my 20 years on the job, I picked up a tuna salad sandwich there for lunch — creature of habit that I am — and glanced at the checkout-stand headlines.

I remember one *National Enquirer* cover in the winter of 2012. It read: "O.J. Bombshell: I'm Khloe's Real Dad." And I remember it because, about an hour later, I was standing near the payphone bank in Phase 1, overhearing O.J. and Khloe passionately debate how to handle the fallout.

I couldn't hear her words, but I knew she was begging him to take a DNA test. O.J. refused, but wouldn't explain why. Then he hung up and turned to me.

"What do you think I should do, Felix?"

Me? WTF?

Once my supervisors at the prison saw the trust O.J. placed in me, they made being his best friend part of my job. They looked the other way when I was late for gun-post duty due to a heart-to-heart in Simpson's cell about his dead sister, or when I couldn't be on the yard because O.J. asked me to do him a personal favor. (I'll get to some of those later.)

This all made perfect sense. If anything ever happened to O.J. — due to something he got up to or a plot hatched by other inmates that he caught wind of – our house would immediately be cleaned from top to bottom. Every officer would be fired. No one's career can survive the intensity of "what went wrong?" media scrutiny like that.

And so I became a super-secret O.J. double agent. Whether I liked it or not, I was his permanent sidekick — the Robin to his Batman, the Jerry to his Tom, the Sundance to his Butch Cassidy. (And I looked it, too, standing only 5-foot-8 to O.J.'s 6-foot-1.) We were inseparable.

Every weekday for seven years, I spent at least 20 minutes a day hanging out with the most famous American ever to be accused of murder. More than 150 million people tuned in to watch O.J. Simpson have that verdict read to him in 1995. Twenty years later, for an hour or more a day, the only one watching him was me. During our conversations, O.J. told me everything about his life.

Everything.

The list of media outlets requesting O.J. interviews was a mile long and got tossed in the garbage every week. The tabloids paid tens of thousands of dollars for information from inmates who weren't close enough to O.J. to spew anything other than facts they made up themselves.

While working at Lovelock, "I cannot confirm or deny that" is all I was permitted to say in response to even the most trivial of O.J. questions. The nondisclosure agreement we all signed to work at Lovelock was so strict, we could not even confirm whether Lovelock was where O.J. was — even though the Nevada

Department of Corrections listed him as an inmate on its website.

When I retired last September, that nondisclosure no longer applied. My prison shackles were unlocked. And so, now, is my strange-but-true story.

Before you start, though, you have my blessing to jump first to the chapter dedicated to O.J.'s penis (Chapter 11, page 74). We both know that's what you were going to do anyway.

This book is for my wife, Rhonda, who seriously worried that I would end up either murdered by O.J. Simpson, or taken as his hostage during a botched escape attempt. Her love for me is rivaled only by her hatred of famous incarcerated former football players.

It's for my sons, Jacob and Zachary, who I couldn't be any prouder of even if they suddenly decided to become prison guards.

And it's for my father, Harvey, for teaching me that living your life for the approval of others is the worst prison of all.

CHAPTER 1:
BRONCO FLASHBACKS

On June 17, 1994, I was watching Hakeem Olajuwon face off against Patrick Ewing on the TV above the bar at the Cheyenne Saloon in Las Vegas, where I bartended and bounced four nights a week for $10 an hour plus tips.

Back then, they never broke into any sports broadcasts to show car chases, much less the NBA playoffs. But there it was.

My first thought was, man, there's a lot of cop cars chasing that Ford Bronco. Why do they need more than three? And why doesn't one of them pin this guy already?

The volume wasn't up loud enough to hear what the reporters were saying, but after a couple of minutes, the screen flashed the words: "LIVE: O.J. SIMPSON IN THE WHITE CAR."

Holy shit. *O.J. Simpson,* one of the greatest football players of all-time and star of the *Naked Gun* movies, was guilty of the murders after all.

What I didn't know was that that Bronco was on a

long and crazy path that would intersect with mine in ways still too bizarre for me to fathom. Exactly 20 years later, I would be watching that same footage again, on the anniversary of its filming. The next time, it would be narrated for me by its star in his prison cell.

"I was really gonna kill myself," O.J. Simpson told me. "The woman I loved most in the whole world was dead and there was no reason for me to live."

He pointed to the dirty 13-inch TV screen, at all the people lining the highways and overpasses. He choked back tears when he saw a little kid holding a sign that read "We love the Juice."

"You see them all cheering for me?" he asked. "They were my inspiration not to commit suicide."

Slinging beer and bouncing assholes was fun. But at 29 years old, I was ready to graduate from bartending. At least I was according to my first wife, who ordered me to get a job with benefits. In Nevada, without a college education, that meant at a casino, a police station or (what sounded like the easiest work to me) a prison.

No little kid answers "prison guard" to "What do you want to be when you grow up?" It just kind of happens. So I found myself sitting in a room taking a written test for the Nevada Department of

Corrections with 15 other guys, second-guessing my decision to quit bartending and wearing a ridiculous wig. (I thought my long bartender hair was prohibited, which it wasn't, and I didn't want to cut it because going back to beerslinging was still an inviting option at this point.)

Nearly 40 percent of test-takers failed. I passed with a score of 70 percent, 12 higher than required. So I moved on to the physical agility test, an obstacle course requiring you to grab a set of keys, run up and down a wooden staircase about 20 feet tall, find and turn the correct key in a lock at the bottom of the stairs back and forth, schlep a 150-lb. dummy 50 feet and drop it, run around a metal pole a few dozen times, then scale a four-foot wooden wall to a 10-foot wooden wall, drop down, run across a balance beam and shimmy through a 20-foot-long cement tunnel.

All in 1 minute and 58 seconds. Oh, and on that particular day, during a blizzard.

My first official job interview was a fake one. I drove up to Ely, Nevada, a town founded as a stagecoach station that hasn't even expanded by 5,000 residents in 100 years since. I knew my wife would never relocate to such a boondocks, so I wasn't there to score a job. Instead, I wrote down the questions the warden asked during our interview. I asked these questions of some guards I found at the city jail back home in Vegas. And then I repeated the answers the first time I was interviewed for a job I was willing to accept.

That was in Lovelock, 120 miles from Carson City, a medium-security prison housing 1,680 offenders and opened in 1995. My scam worked perfectly. The interviewers were blown away that I knew that, if an inmate climbed a fence while I manned a gun tower, the procedure was to verbally warn the inmate to stop and, if the inmate didn't comply, to aim for the inmate's center of mass and shoot. And they loved that I threw in the words "firm," "fair" and "consistent" when they asked what kind of corrections officer I would be.

All went exactly according to my evil plan. Until my wife flew up with me to move.

"You better hope Carson City's bigger than Reno," she said as we landed in Reno and looked around. (It's not. It's actually less than a quarter of the size, with only 55,000 residents.)

She then asked how much money I had, and demanded that I give her all $500. She drove the rental car back to Las Vegas and told me I had 90 days to transfer down to Las Vegas.

What a gal. I can't believe I let her get away.

CHAPTER 2:
WHAT IT'S LIKE
TO GUARD A PRISON

Imagine the exact same routine. Every hour of every day. Until you retire. That's prison-guarding. You and 50 other guards watching 1,700 inmates essentially do nothing all day but move from building to building. When I heard the radio key up at 10:42 a.m., I knew what was about to be announced: "S&E law library, legal mail is ready." (That's short for Search and Escort.) Same thing with chow in the morning. At 5:52, they'd announce: "Unit 6, send your early chow and your workers to breakfast."

But prison-guarding isn't all interminable boredom. Occasionally, there is also sheer panic. And you kind of welcome it for breaking the monotony. One night, Lovelock hosted its own unintentional re-enactment of the Mexican-Indian Wars. Our Mexican and Native American populations had been building up tension for weeks — all over one guy disrespecting another guy in the chow hall. You can imagine how stupid it gets sometimes.

I was up in Gun Post 4, waiting for the gym to

open, kicking back and eating my food. The radio shouted: "We've got a 1010 on the yard!" That was code for a fight. (The FCC did away with codes years ago.) Actually, there were multiple fights. It was everywhere, shotguns firing. I ran over the roof to Gun Post 2, which overlooks the Phase 1 yard, for a closer peek. More than 50 Mexicans were getting the crap beaten out of them by only 30 Native Americans, who were not only huge but possessed.

Suddenly, all four main unit doors swung open and 250 Mexicans flew out. All I could figure was that the officers in the bubble opened them to let their men enter the yard and control the situation, without regard for the consequences. So 250 Mexicans were swarming 30 Native Americans. The Mexicans actually fought *each other* to get to the Native Americans.

I yelled "Get on the ground!" and "Stop fighting!" Then I shot, but nothing happened. I looked in my shotgun. No shells! They were in my gun post for the gym! That's how rare an incident like this was. (By the way, the Native Americans were *still* holding their own. They were getting pummeled, but refused to go down.)

So I slung my shotgun and ran like a dog. I got my little box of shells, loaded five in and ran back and ... it was over. The lieutenant was on the yard, putting zip ties on all the inmates. He looked at me and yelled, "Where the hell have you been?"

I couldn't tell him what really happened, because that would have gotten me 30 days suspension. So I told him I was on the toilet (a convenient excuse for a lot of prison-guard wrongdoing, it turns out). Then there was the near riot that happened in front of culinary, the day the inmates decided they didn't want to use sporks that were washed and reused – only disposable sporks. After the shift sergeant couldn't convince the inmates to disperse, the lieutenant decided it would be a great time for the new K-9 officers to release their huge German Shepherds with the attack command.

Only one tiny oversight: The dogs were trained on guards since we couldn't have them attacking inmates for practice. So all three dogs ran straight past the protesting inmates and after the three of us officers. I dropped my duty belt and ran for my life. Two of the cujos chased me up a fence and tried to bite my feet.

The K-9 detail was disbanded immediately after that. Frankly, I was surprised. Since the prison already paid for and trained the dogs, I figured they would keep them. I mean, in the end, their first mission was a complete success: The inmates stopped protesting and fell to the ground. Because they were doubling over with laughter.

Other times, I created my own drama just to entertain myself. Which explains why I can no longer bend the middle finger on my right hand.

Let's just say that the Aryans in Unit 2A were none too pleased with being overseen by Nevada's only Jewish prison guard. And, I don't know, but maybe I asked them one too many times if everything was "kosher."

The mistake I made on this day was tapping on their cell as part of my taunt. Any good guard manning the locks will interpret this as a request to pop the door. And, unfortunately, there was a good guard manning the locks.

So I ran from the freshly popped mob seeking my death, as anyone possessing combined senses of intelligence and their own mortality would, the vision of my dead uncle at the end of a long tunnel of light. I made it out the cellblock door, which is why you're reading this right now, but not far enough so that the Aryans couldn't slam the door in the gate so severely, I passed out and have a tough time hitting the "u" on my computer keyboard.

CHAPTER 3:
INMATE NO. 1027820

"Well just outside of nowhere
Mile marker 105.
You'll find yourself in Lovelock
Where the game is to stay alive."

– "Limbo in Lovelock," Hot Buttered Rum

I had some practice dealing with incarcerated sports stars. In 1999, former WBA heavyweight champ Michael Dokes received 4-15 years after being convicted of attacking his fiancé. Based on my experience, I'd have to guess that conviction correct. At least that's the impression I got when Dokes tried to introduce his famous right hook to my face.

Even for a prison inmate, Dokes was having a bummer of a time. He had health issues, no money, and he had given away four houses that he owned to friends so he wouldn't lose them. And, as soon as he got his out date — what do you know? —

friends stopped returning his phone calls. I knew all this because he told me his life story once or twice. We were buddies — until I thanked him for losing a 1988 fight to Evander Holyfield that won my father a crap-ton of money. Actually, I may have thanked him for "throwing the fight."

Hey, he was an old man and I was bored and wanted to see what would happen. Well, I got my wish and, had I not ducked out of the way quickly enough, he would never have gotten paroled when he did in 2008. (Of course, I probably also would have gotten my retirement a decade early, but that didn't occur to me until later.)

I didn't report Dokes because I was totally being a dick and didn't want to rat myself out. Instead, I decided to have some more fun with him. I went up to the TV room, where they screen movies and old sporting events. I found the inmate in charge and instructed him to screen the Holyfield-Dokes fight 24 hours a day all weekend. If anyone complained, I told him, let them know it was on my orders.

At 7:30 Monday morning, Dokes marched right for me as I entered the yard. I looked up at the gun post to make sure I was covered. What I didn't expect is for him to reach into his pocket for something. Shit, I was about to get shanked.

What he pulled out was a white cloth. He waved it

and we shook hands.

Until seven years ago, I thought my boxing match against Michael Dokes would be the story of my career, the one I would bore my grandchildren with as they push me away due to my old-man breath.

Boy, was I wrong.

The laundry officer gets a list of all the new inmates every day, and yep. I mean, we knew O.J. Simpson had to be incarcerated somewhere in Nevada, because that's where he decided to commit his latest crime. (O.J. was found guilty of multiple felony charges for leading a group of men into a room at Las Vegas' Palace Station Hotel in September 2007, where they attempted to steal sports memorabilia that O.J. thought was rightfully his. Two of the men testified that they brought guns at O.J.'s request.)

But I guess the possibility never seemed entirely real.

When O.J. was sentenced to 22 years in prison in December 2008, he was remanded to High Desert State Prison in Indian Springs, about 30 miles north of Las Vegas. Three days into his stay, however, they started firing lieutenants. I heard it was a booking photo that got leaked out in some of their emails. Whatever it was, it was clear the warden didn't want O.J. there; it meant way too much drama for him. So he was shipped as far away from civilization as possible.

And so, O.J. Simpson traveled in a single van down to Lovelock in the middle of the night. No one knew it was happening. Usually, a transfer will be on the board in the sergeant's office. But this is the one time no one knew, not even the sergeant. The mission was called "Secret Squirrel Shit," I learned later.

As soon as the decision was made to ship him to Lovelock, every employee was forced to sign a nondisclosure agreement under threat of dismissal. The agreement didn't mention O.J. by name, referring just to anyone of "celebrity status." But we knew what it meant.

Lovelock Correctional Center is about seven miles outside Lovelock, a town of about 2,000 in desolate Pershing County, Nevada. Two miles in one direction is a beautiful and treacherously impassible mountain range, two miles in the opposite direction is Interstate 80. It's a medium-security prison to most of its 1,680 inmates, but there are many close-custody segregation inmates and a separate unit that houses some minimum-custody prisoners.

At first, O.J. was isolated in our infirmary, as a safety precaution. Then he was moved to the general population, into an 80-square-foot cell – one of the biggest: Unit 6A, 64B, bottom bunk. That is one of the worker units, one of the most lenient residences that can be scored in Lovelock. Another name for Unit 6a is the Country Club.

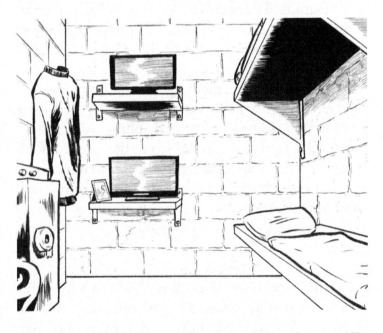

Unit 6A has no floor officer to shake down cells and make inmates miserable during compliance checks. There is only a single unit control officer who opens and shuts doors and provides gun coverage. The gym workers have their own bathroom area and a back room where they check out equipment to the other inmates for racquetball games, basketball and weight-lifting. In fact, because prison workers must be among the first to open a prison back up after lockdown, they are even sometimes able to ignore the lockdown.

In exchange for this lenient existence, O.J. was given a job: sweeping and mopping the basketball court floor, wiping off the Universal weight gym, and cleaning the coach's office and bathroom for an hour from Tuesday to Friday. Some of the jobs at the gym pay, but not O.J.'s.

The gym is where I met O.J. for the first time. He was standing there in the gray sweats, dark-blue state-issued winter coat and blue ball cap he purchased from the inmate store. (People think all inmates wear orange all the time. But that's only in maximum-security prisons. In minimum- and medium-security, they're in blue unless they're being moved or in segregation or protective custody.)

He introduced himself as "Juice," which is both his yard name and what friends call him on the outside. Not everyone gets to determine his own yard name. But it's a measure of respect when you do, and O.J. did. He called me *sir*, which I hated. I told him to knock it off, that I was no better than him. (Well, at least outside the eyes of the law I wasn't.) And I was just Felix from then onward.

O.J. then excused himself, bent down and finished

his pretend-golf game. He would pretend-golf a lot. Every day, in fact. Since you can't be issued a golf club for obvious reasons, he imagined one was always with him. It appeared to be a nine iron.

I then told the Juice I heard who he was rooming with and asked who the man was in their relationship. (O.J.'s first cellie was a serial rapist. More on that later.) This is not a moment I'm particularly proud of. But hey, I never knew I'd be writing a book and it's the truth.

O.J. stared at me like I was nuts. "There's no relationship," he said. He appeared to be really upset. But after a few seconds, he smiled and the ice was broken.

You can understand how I gained O.J. Simpson's trust by understanding the different approaches there are to prison-guarding. Some guards get off on being hard-asses. One guy who comes to mind is a super-fat guard the inmates referred to as "Petty Sergeant" because he constantly threatened to write up inmates for untucked shirts, non-immaculate beds and having three rolls of toilet paper instead of the maximum allowance of two. (Sometimes the night officer just hands out extra TP so he only has to do it once a week.)

Douchebags like this think that's how to earn respect. And they do earn a certain type of respect. But it's the kind where you're constantly looking over your shoulder. Can you imagine trying to maintain that level of vigilance for an entire career? Petty Sergeant will find many more grievances filed against him than his co-workers, which the warden and other higher-ups do not like to deal with.

Obviously, I fell on the opposite spectrum end. A prison guard's job is to prevent escapes, to protect staff from inmates, to protect inmates from inmates, and to protect state property. It is *not* to punish inmates. Sentences already do that. Prisoners are confined to a cage, have no free will to come and go and do as they please, and are separated from their loved ones and their constitutional rights sometimes until they die. Sometimes, they're even raped and won't report it for fear of being killed. These guys have already ruined their lives by making bad decisions. It's not my job to make things worse for them.

My thing was to minimize drama and inmates challenging my authority. Look, guys, don't try and escape around me. But if you want to have consensual sex or make homemade "pruno" wine, you know what? Just don't let me catch you. When it was my turn to conduct shakedowns, I jangled my keys so everyone knew I was coming. Sometimes, I even made a ridiculous announcement: "Attention on the tier, Officer Felix will now be doing a compliance check."

Not long after I met O.J., I spotted a fantasy football sheet sitting on the shelf in his cell. O.J. was big-time into fantasy football. He even ordered the weekly magazine *Fantasy Football.* A hard-ass guard would have written him up for the betting sheet. But I just copied all his picks down and used them for my Yahoo Sports Fantasy Football league online. I mean, who knows more about football than a Heisman trophy winner? As it turns out, O.J.'s picks (and mine) won for three years in a row. (O.J. caught on after I kept asking him whether I should keep or replace the same exact players he picked, and he thought it was funny.)

But O.J.'s arrival opened up the split between the hard-asses and the good prison employees into an earthquake-sized fault. About a third of my co-workers believed part of their job was to punish O.J. for the double-murders he got away with 20 years earlier, and there was no gray area on this subject. Even the free staff workers in culinary, the clinic, canteen and laundry all fell in one of the two camps.

The tension got so bad, it even split up carpools. A couple of vehicles rode out from Reno, a couple from Fernley and a couple from Fallon, Nevada, every day. About a month after O.J.'s arrival, the passengers reshuffled their vehicles according to O.J. stance. One of the vans that carpooled from Reno began calling itself the "Goldman Van." While the guys I rode in with would talk about normal daily events, passengers in the Goldman Van would emerge talking about creative ways to harass O.J. as they stared us down. Their goal was to screw with the guy mentally and physically, and to write him disciplinaries that would ruin his chances at parole.

Once, at the cattle guard – a piece of farm equipment a quarter mile from the prison where employees could fight without being on state property — a fistfight erupted between an anti-O.J. guard and a caseworker who was sick enough of his bullshit to finally speak up. (The caseworker beat the guard's ass.)

I wasn't there, but I heard about a guard trainee working in O.J.'s unit who received a phone call. It was from an anti-O.J. officer impersonating a sergeant. The trainee was ordered to not only search O.J.'s cell, but to tear it apart. O.J. stood outside, waiting calmly, as the trainee did as he was told. Another phone call, again from the impostor, interrupted the trainee, informing him that he "did the Goldmans a solid." It took O.J. three hours to put his cell back together.

The warden is supposed to monitor and address potential trigger situations like this. But the problem was that there were four shifts in the prison: Day A, Day B, Night A and Night B. Each shift worked 12 hours, which meant there were four different lieutenants and four different sergeants running the shifts – each one differently. And the warden didn't work nights or weekends.

I admit falling on the *extremely* friendly end of the inmate-friendly prison guards. I always found that befriending inmates helped me do my job better. *Much* better. And that's because inmates know *everything,* and they know it before we do. They're everywhere and they live to gossip. Once, an inmate told me my days off were changing. I told him, "You don't know what you're talking about." But he was 100 percent right. Another inmate told me a sergeant was out to get me. And he was. He was thinking of writing me up for a bogus sick leave.

We had an inmate working in operations, yard-named Catfish, who would put a cup to the walls when they had meetings in the lieutenant's office. For as long as he worked in operations — which wasn't long! — I knew *everything* happening in that prison. I'd have my little two minutes with him and he would mention everyone who was being investigated.

It didn't surprise me that prison management quickly took notice of my friendship with O.J. (How could they not? There were cameras everywhere and O.J. made a beeline for me whenever I walked onto the yard.) In the beginning, if our conversations made me late for my duty at a post, I was reprimanded by my sergeant, who saw O.J.'s interest in hanging with me as a prison liability.

However, someone above him soon realized that this friendship was something to be encouraged. Because if the slightest harm ever came to O.J., or if O.J. ever inflicted the slightest harm on anyone else, all my supervisors would be fired. Most prison officials I've met want to do the right thing for their inmates and the greater good of society, but none gets to do these things if they don't also get to keep their jobs.

After a few months, the reprimands stopped. And, while it was never spelled out to me, I realized what the deal was... If O.J. Simpson was trying to pull or hide something, it was my job to let my superior officers know about it before it happened.

CHAPTER 4:
WHITE BLOODY GLOVE TREATMENT

Every prisoner at Lovelock is treated equally. At least, that's what the prisoners are told. Nothing can be further from the truth, however, when their ranks include someone with such a high profile. In fact, having O.J. Simpson at Lovelock changed pretty much every rule we had. And that's because it altered the behavior of the guards, compromising their integrity, their ethics and their training.

One guard got fired almost immediately for looking up O.J.'s ID card in our computer, printing out a copy and taking it home. Another covering in the mailroom got suspended for opening letters to O.J. from one of the Kardashians. (I never could find out for sure which, but my guess is Khloe or Kim.) The letters expressed concern over his weight, begging him to shed 20 lbs. lest he suffer a medical problem in prison.

Below are some of the hard-and-fast rules I call the O.J. Exceptions. I'm positive that even O.J. won't have realized the full scope of his special treatment until he reads this.

O.J. Exception 1: If an altercation on the yard requires shots to be fired, O.J. cannot get hit.

In other words, if O.J. decides to hold an inmate, guard or even the warden hostage, he must either be physically subdued without the use of a firearm, talked out of it, or given what he wants.

O.J. Exception 2: Any use of force against O.J. must be authorized by the sergeant on duty or higher.

So physically restraining O.J. cannot be a spur-of-the-moment decision. Taking this to its logical conclusion boggles the mind... Basically, O.J. can get away with any behavior he wants if there is no sergeant or higher officer on duty or immediately reachable. This includes escaping. *He must be allowed to escape.* (There is always supposed to be sergeant on duty, by the way, but still....)

O.J. Exception 3: No inmate can work a job for more than two years except for Prison Industries employees and O.J. Simpson.

This rule was adopted about five years ago to protect the staff and officers in any one prison area from becoming overly friendly and compromised. It placed a lot of pressure on the working inmates since jobs provide good days (up to 10 day credits a month toward an early release) to all of them and a steady source of income to some. But it's the exceptions to the rule that really made some inmates seethe. O.J. got to keep his cushy gym job as long as he wants, since he likes it and it's caused no trouble so far. (Prison Industries is a more rigorously monitored sector where the state sells prison labor to the public and private industry in specialized areas: clothing manufacture, auto repair, welding, woodworking, etc.)

O.J. Exception 4: O.J. is the only inmate with direct access to the warden.

The warden is directly responsible for O.J.'s health and welfare. In other words, if O.J. feels mistreated by a guard or other prison employee, or has any complaint at all, he gets the big guy's first available calendar appointment. This unheard-of right is akin to a U.S. Army soldier being allowed to meet with the President of the United States anytime he feels like it. Even Sgt. Elvis Presley couldn't do that.

O.J. Exception 5: Unit 6A is first on line for everything.

Worker units always go before other inmates units for chow, pills and other privileges. But before O.J.'s arrival, they always switched off so that each had a crack at being first. That policy disappeared so that the officers and phase sergeant could personally observe O.J. and check his physical and mental welfare, reporting anything out of the ordinary to their superiors. (In addition, deliveries from Carson City Pharmacy must always be checked first for O.J. Simpson's correct medication.)

O.J. Exception 6: No unscheduled visitor contact with O.J. Simpson.

When visitors tour the prison, none are allowed to tour Unit 6A. And if O.J. happens to be on the yard during a tour – most likely the result of scheduling miscalculation — the guide is instructed to steer clear of O.J. and not to point him out.

O.J. Exception 7: Unit 6A must stand for the health-and-welfare count.

If O.J.'s neighbors ever figured out that they alone were ordered to stand for this 6:45 a.m. routine, and they wondered why, it's because the guards are making sure that O.J. feels well enough to stand up. It is possible to suffer a stroke while sitting down and looking perfectly healthy. And if you're just a Joe Schmoe convict, that's not really the prison's concern.

O.J. Exception 8: All prison guards and inmates must carry an ID card except O.J. Simpson.

After the guard was fired for copying O.J.'s ID card, O.J.'s ID no longer showed up in our computer system and O.J. no longer carried a physical card around with him. Who in the prison couldn't immediately identify him? In one of his rare reflective moods, the Juice once told me: "When I walk into a room, I want people to know who I am. I've always been like that." In a sick way, being incarcerated is actually his dream come true.

O.J. Simpson is allowed to walk into exit doors and cut the lines for chow and meds. And he is also the only prisoner I've ever seen with gym time all to himself. This is basically because O.J. creates a security risk. Whenever he's just standing around doing nothing, a crowd will gather and want to talk to him about football. Or movies. Or the Bronco chase. And suddenly, everybody's forgetting the rules and laughing and getting loud.

As you can imagine, this privilege didn't go over well with the anti-O.J. officers. They hated him already, and now they had to be his servant?

This is why it wasn't unusual for O.J. to be walking to work, the clinic or to culinary and have gates clank closed right in front of him. Sometimes, the guard would ask O.J. for a secret password he was never issued. He told me this would happen three or four times a week, although I've only seen it a couple of times. (I'm sure the other guards realize not to do it around me.)

The password would be something like "Fred Goldman," "Ron Goldman," "Nicole Brown Simpson" or "Marcia Clark." Eventually, O.J. caught on and would use all these names until he hit the right one. After opening the gate, the officer would call the next gun-post officer to close the next gate on O.J. and ask him for the same password. Or change it to a new one related to the double-murders.

The resentments built up by some inmates were just as intense. Whenever a tabloid reported something negative about O.J. — an altercation, hunger strike or illegal sexual encounter — the director instructed the warden to personally check on O.J.'s welfare and get the story straight. (Most of the time, these stories were made up, but it didn't matter. They still needed to be checked out.) Inmates *hate* when the warden enters their unit since certain infractions would always be seen that needed to be addressed. It's about as welcome a thing as when the principal entered your high-school classroom.

Sometimes, inmate hatred toward O.J. would boil over. Three years ago, a neo-Nazi with a history of violence spoke up when O.J. cut him on the pill line, cutting back in front of him and telling him to get "his ugly black ass" to the back of the line and wait like everyone else.

Travis Waugh was never supposed to be in a pill line with O.J. But one of the newer officers mistakenly let his maximum-security unit mix with O.J.'s. Shit happens.

Waugh's comment prompted the closest thing to a fit I've even heard of O.J. throwing in his seven captive years.

"Fuck you!" he yelled. "I'm gonna stay right here and your ass ain't gonna do nothing about it!"

Waugh then pushed O.J., knocking him off his cane and onto the floor. O.J. then rushed Waugh and spit in his face before other inmates began holding them both back and Waugh issued a colorful death threat featuring the n-word.

"I did it again," O.J. told me the next morning, on the verge of crying. "I screwed up."

So I tried smoothing things out, which is in the best interest both of O.J. and the prison. I went to see Waugh but was told to get the hell out of his cell or my ass would be beaten. Normally, you write an inmate up for threatening you. But that would have left this one still intent on harming O.J. So I went to the alleged shot-caller of the Aryans and threatened to transfer him to Ely, where three feet of snow had just fallen, if he didn't make Waugh shake O.J.'s hand. Of course, I didn't have the power to make a transfer. But I could have built the case that this inmate was the shot-caller, something my bosses had yet to prove at the time.

Within 30 minutes, Waugh and O.J. were shaking hands.

CHAPTER 5:
JEW-JUICE TIME

"Jew-Juice time!" O.J. called out to me. That's what he called our chats, which usually occurred while walking circles around Lovelock's 50-yard race track or in O.J.'s cell. He told me I was his favorite Jew ever, which I didn't mind. It was flipped positive, the way some inmates call each other the n-word.

This particular Jew-Juice time was important to O.J., I could tell. He walked at me harder than usual, without his usual smile, before we began circling the track.

There was a guard working in Unit 1 that seemed to get off on harassing the Juice. He would constantly order O.J. to produce his ID card, knowing full well he was not issued one. After giving the explanation for the hundredth time, O.J. would then be grilled about his knowledge of drugs and sports betting on the yard. And the guard would call him "boy" while all this was happening, as he would all black inmates. This was usually followed by some variation on "I know your black butt is up to something."

O.J. asked me what could be done. I couldn't speak directly to this guard because – surprise, surprise! – this racist hated Jews as well as blacks. So I reported him to the warden, who always welcomed information I brought to him about O.J.'s state of mind.

The racist guard was given the choice of being investigated for racism or transferring to a prison camp 40 miles away. He chose the camp.

This led to a transformation in my friendship with O.J. Back in his cell, awaiting his new cellie, he hugged me and assured me of a place in his inner circle.

"If I ever get out of here," he said, "you and me are golfing together every weekend."

I never lost sight of the dark side of my new BFF. O.J. Simpson is a heinous criminal. There is no doubt in my mind that he murdered two innocent people and all but ruined the lives of everyone they touched — including his own children. And on the slim chance that he didn't murder Nicole Brown Simpson and Ronald Goldman himself, I'll bet the farm that he was at least involved or knew who did it.

Yet, at the same time, I'm not going to deny how cool it felt to have the ear of one of my childhood idols on a daily basis — to have the second-leading all-time football rusher advise me on how to deal with my disapproving father, the star of *Naked Gun* tell me which cars are the most reliable. (And no, he didn't say Fords!) How to handle being star-struck was not part of the job training for $25/hour prison guards in Middle-of-Nowhere, Nevada.

And so I did the worst thing imaginable for a guard: I let my guard down. I let O.J. inside my head. But it wasn't just about being star-struck. O.J. Simpson is the most model prisoner I ever met in my 20 years as a prison guard. He treats everybody he encounters with respect and warmth, never talks down or flies off the handle, and regularly helps de-escalate problems between other inmates. He referees softball and basketball games and is the only prisoner I've ever known to resist gossip and shit-talking. The O.J. Simpson I knew is what my people would call a real *mensch*. If you had no idea who he was in the past, you would have no qualms inviting him over to dine with your family once he got out.

About five years ago, O.J. caught an inmate in his cell looking around for something to steal. This guy was a known cell thief, someone who was shunned on the yard for it. Instead of slugging him, yelling at him, or calling me, O.J. sat him down and asked him to explain himself. The guy had no money coming in from the streets and his job had no pay number. He was broke and hungry. O.J. took him to the canteen and bought him a bunch of stuff, whatever he wanted. He mentored the guy, took him to church and hung out with him on the yard, listening to his problems.

O.J. didn't do this to gain points with the guards or

his parole board. He never mentioned what happened and none of us even knew until O.J. asked if I could get this guy a job. (I got him an interview that landed him a job in Prison Industries and he worked out well.)

Another inmate approached O.J. in church to admit contemplating suicide. He figured O.J. could relate because, well, the Bronco chase. Rather than report the inmate and get him placed on suicide watch, O.J. orchestrated an intervention with some of his Christian friends. The Juice explained the wonderful relationship he has with his kids now and how that wouldn't be the case if he killed himself back in 1994.

O.J. did some research and found out the inmate's young daughter visits him every month. No matter how bad things get, O.J. told the inmate, committing suicide would mess that little girl up for life.

"That visit with you means the world to your daughter," he said, "and you want to take away her world?"

After he became a part of my everyday life, I read up a lot on O.J. Simpson. I would wait until my wife fell asleep and sift through what newspaper reporters, police officers and bloggers had to say about his violence, his character. I wanted to know if my own life was in danger. One of the things I learned was that when O.J. was inducted into the Pro Football Hall of Fame in 1985, his own mother, Eunice Simpson, gave a speech that included this statement: "He always said, 'One of these days you're going to read about me.' And my oldest daughter would always say, `In the police report.' "

This wasn't O.J.'s first incarceration, either. Growing up in San Francisco's tough Potrero Hill housing projects, he and A.C. Cowlings were in a street gang, and O.J. got a taste of his distant future in the city's juvenile detention center for a weekend. He was 15 and the Persian Warriors were caught stealing liquor from a convenience store.

Said O.J. once: "It wasn't a weekend if there wasn't a fight ... I enjoyed it."

The next day, I would go to work and this totally different guy would hug me hello.

Every time a guard or another inmate harassed O.J., a part of me expected to witness an explosively violent reaction, some back-breaking straw that finally caused his true inner murderer to re-emerge. But that part of me grew smaller and smaller because nothing ever happened. O.J. always played along, never losing his cool.

Of course, O.J. is an actor and can play *the part* of a good human being. But, let's face it, he doesn't have an Academy Award for a reason. There's a difference between memorizing a few lines for a summer blockbuster and living 24/7 inside a goldfish bowl, your every move monitored by other human beings, as a completely peaceful person.

It is absolutely *impossible* to reconcile Mensch O.J. with Monster O.J. You know that these diametrically opposed people both exist, that they're both very real and inhabit the same body. And yet they just don't square at all. It's like trying to watch a rerun of *The Cosby Show* now.

And so, for me, resolving this tension meant learning to see O.J. as neither mensch nor monster. To me, he was more like a Dr. Jekyll who decided to stop drinking magic potions ... after it was already too late to matter. Just because he no longer transformed into Mr. Hyde didn't change what happened or absolve him of any responsibility for what Mr. Hyde did. But it did make it easier for me to do my job and enjoy this beyond-surreal situation.

CHAPTER 6:
LIKE FATHER, UNLIKE SON

Harvey Felix wasn't a bad father. I mean, he loved me, even though neither of us have ever said the words to each other. He managed all my little league teams and coached my basketball teams growing up. He's just a guy with issues. And I can understand them, considering what he went through in his own childhood.

O.J. Simpson isn't my only connection to an American sports figure. My dad's father was Barney Felix, the referee who called the 1964 boxing match that introduced the world to the future Muhammad Ali. Cassius Clay, his name then, was a 7:1 underdog against Sonny Liston, the reigning powerhouse who, in that ring, under my grandfather's watch, would be reduced to embarrassing obscurity.

To my dad, however, Barney Felix was only an asshole. He cheated on my grandmother, then left her with no money and two kids to raise on her own. My dad was 8 at the time. And I blame Barney's actions for all the problems Harvey had as a father. You just don't get over trauma that deep.

Unlike Barney, Harvey made sure to always be there for me, and I credit him for that. However, the love I felt from him was conditional. Basically, he was embarrassed to have a prison guard for a son. A doctor, a lawyer, a cop? Fine. ANYTHING more respectable.

Harvey chose a prestigious career for himself that ensured everyone knew his name. He ran the Centers for Disease Control for the West Coast, so it was his mug on TV whenever a health issue cropped up. VD? Swine flu? My dad popped up with all the info.

It was very important, I believe, for him to earn the love from his community that his own dad wouldn't show him, to fill the hole he saw every time he looked at that empty dining-room chair and wondered why. And this same insecurity, I think, made him see me with an equally prestigious career – or at least one requiring more than a high-school education and no felonies.

Nearly every weekday morning for the past decade, my dad has gone to his local McDonald's to meet with 10 friends who also retired from prestigious careers. He tells me stories about them. I know every guy. One's a retired Detroit crop with lots of street sense. My dad refers to him as "the smartest guy in the world." There's also a retired UNLV professor, a veteran of WWII who fought on the beach at Normandy and another retired cop from back east. Dad calls it "McDonald's Club."

My own two teenage boys were invited to sit in on McDonald's Club once, as was my wife. But never me. Once, I drove over and peered in through the plate-glass window, trying to place the names with the faces. (Holy shit, did I just admit that in a book?)

Look, my dad is now 80 years old and he'll probably tell you this little theory of mine is 100 percent bullshit. Guys from that generation don't believe in expressing their feelings — or even in therapy. Frankly, I've had more heart-to-hearts with O.J. than my dad.

But it really sucks to have a father who isn't proud of you. Trying to change that is the reason I've bought him big-screen TVs for Father's Day. I don't even buy my mother a card. I just call her and tell her I love her. Yet my dad, he gets 50" Vizios. If my wife hadn't stopped me one birthday, I might have bought him the car I had picked out for him.

Many times, my dad told me I should have finished college and went to law or med school. He offered to pay. I told him I wasn't interested. He took it as a personal insult.

When my sons ask me what they should be when they grow up, I tell them happy. I put no conditions on my love. It turns out that both of them want to be registered nurses, and I couldn't be prouder of them!

I remember the first time I brought McDonald's Club up to O.J. It was not long after my boys attended, and the Juice could sense something troubling me.

"Can I hug you?" O.J. asked me.

"When I get out," he promised me, "I'm going to walk right into the next McDonald's Club with you."

Then he dropped a hydrogen bomb onto the conversation.

"At least your dad wasn't a drag queen who died of AIDS."

What the what?

Jimmy Lee Simpson left his family when O.J. was four years old. He worked as a chef at Alioto's Italian restaurant on Fisherman's Wharf, and as a janitor in a bank, and publicly crossdressed during his time off. As I listened to O.J. describe their troubled relationship, my own complaints melted away into the background.

"It made me angry," O.J. told me of the updates he would get about his dad from the kids at school. "'Hey, I saw your other mommy in his dress last weekend in the Mission District!'"

Jimmy never came out as gay. You just didn't in the 1950s. Even in San Francisco. But O.J. heard he was dating a waiter at Alioto's. He also suspected him of being a drug abuser.

O.J.'s mom always stuck up for his dad. She told him he had a good heart but was confused. Nevertheless, on the many occasions that Jimmy reached out, O.J. wanted nothing to do with him.

"He was a disappointment to me," he said, "an embarrassment."

It wasn't until Jimmy lay dying of AIDS in 1986 that O.J. came around – at the behest, of course, of his mom.

In the hospital, Jimmy told his famous son he was very proud of him for graduating from USC. He seemed more impressed by his college graduation than his NFL career, O.J. told me, since it had always been a dream of Jimmy's to graduate college.

Cutting his dad out until the end of his life is one of O.J.'s biggest regrets. And it explains O.J.'s advice to me.

"Don't hold a grudge against your dad," he said. "He has his reasons for being the way he is. Go to him while you still can."

CHAPTER 7:
MEET THE CELLIES

Cellie # 1
Israel Fields
Yard name: "Izzy"

A 6-foot-9 monster who stared at the world with a lazy left eye, Izzy worked for me in Prison Industries. He once described to me what he was in for as "a lot of rapes." When I asked what qualified as "a lot" in the rape world, he replied "more than 100" and I took a step backward.

I have no idea why Lovelock officials thought a serial rapist the perfect first roommate match for O.J. Simpson. Perhaps these were the two prisoners they were trying the hardest to protect from other inmates, and keeping them together meant less work. Or perhaps someone in administration had a sense of karmic justice about Bundy Drive.

A lot of guards hated Izzy. Not because he was a rapist or anything, but because he was a law clerk, which is kind of worse than a serial rapist to them. Whenever an inmate gets written up by a guard, a law clerk is who represents the inmate against the guard. And the guards don't like that at all.

But O.J. got along surprisingly well with Izzy, who took him under his wing and taught him the prison ropes. Izzy especially enjoyed playing pranks on O.J. The best was when he told his cellie that the property room had just stopped by and requested that he report there immediately, with his TV, to verify that it's his name and prisoner number on the back of it.

So O.J. walks across the yard carrying this old-timey RCA 13-inch TV and the inmates are like, "Where is the Juice going with that TV?" The gun-post officer approached him and, in the five minutes it took for the guard to get a handle on the situation and break the news to O.J. that he had been played, Izzy had clued the entire yard in on the prank. So when O.J. walked back to his cell with his TV, explosive laughter ensued. It was the reddist I had ever seen O.J.'s face.

The truth is, Izzy was a teddy bear. A big, raping teddy bear.

Unfortunately for O.J., Izzy had a medical condition that warranted his transfer to the Regional Medical Facility, which is pretty much the Nevada Department of Corrections' version of South Florida: you go there to die. I can't say what his medical condition was, but Izzy had a lazy eye that he told me resulted from a medical procedure performed in prison.

Cellie #2
Willie Hartwell
Yard name: "Smoke"

Smoke was 44 years old, 6-feet tall, 180 pounds and bad-ass. In 2002, he was sentenced to 10-25 years for armed robbery with a deadly weapon. (Kidnapping charges were plea-bargained away.) And, as impossible as it might be to believe, this was not Smoke's first offense. (Shocking, I know!)

O.J. hired Smoke as a bodyguard. The job paid $150 a week in goods from the canteen, the money from an NFL pension that neither the government nor Fred Goldman could intercept.

You might think that O.J. Simpson wouldn't need a prison bodyguard. For the most part, you'd be right. To men who live in a cage, release comes only in the form of shitty food, shitty employment and shitty companionship. How can a typical day like theirs not be brightened by a chance hallway Q&A about what it was like on the set of *Naked Gun* or how it felt rushing for a record 273 yards? O.J. Simpson was one of the biggest sports and movie stars in history. Now he was just another inmate to bump into on the yard after lunch.

But some prisoners — a very small but troubling minority — weren't having any of it. They wanted to cause as much trouble for their famous jailmate as they could — either out of a desire for their own personal infamy, because they couldn't stand the prison perks that O.J. got and they didn't, or because they wanted to try and get something off him.

Smoke's job eventually transcended bodyguard into personal assistant. He would get his famous cellmate's food for him from the canteen, and cook it back in their cell. He'd boil Ramen noodles, fry eggs and mash potatoes. He'd microwave the fried chicken O.J. paid $11 for at the prison store, along with the seven strips of bacon that cost $8.

Both O.J. and Smoke had it made. O.J. enjoyed the freedom to stroll around the yard, or sit on the bench while coaching the softball team and eating ice-cream sandwiches, without concern for his safety because Smoke was right there to fend off any troublemakers.

Smoke lived like a king, with all the extra food, toiletries, magazines and stamps he could ever dream of.

And then, as usual, greed had to go and spoil the party. This time, its name was Daniel Lee, a Unit 2 inmate yard-named Honeybun. (And, if you saw this guy, you would realize how ironically conferred that yard name was.) Honeybun caught wind of the O.J./Smoke industry and saw his own dollar signs. Agreeing to split some of the blackmailing profit with Smoke, he convinced them to demand $150 a week of his own in canteen goods, or else he and Smoke would "take care of" O.J., who didn't seek an in-depth explanation of exactly what that meant.

In prison, dealing with a bully is a real Catch-22 situation. Fighting, regardless of who starts or is right, automatically lands you in the hole and dings your record. It's just never smart. Plus, in his late 60s, O.J. was not in the shape he used to be. He could probably still land a damaging shot, but throwing it places him in the bad position of not only getting severely punished by the administration, but also possibly severely beaten.

In prison, you can't have your friends fight your battles for you, because that makes you weak. And you *definitely* can't report a bully to officials, because that makes you a rat. And that's not something you ever want to be in even the cushiest of behind-bar situations.

"What's my play, Felix?" O.J. asked me. Even though it's been 35 years since O.J. played pro ball, his speech was still peppered with football talk.

I had a solution, and it wasn't too uncommon a protocol breach. I slid an anonymous note implicating Smoke and Honeybun into the inmate investigator's mail slot. (There are no cameras in the operations office.)

It couldn't have been a big secret that I wrote the note. The investigator must have known it came from a guard, since no one else had access. And who, other than his favorite guard, would O.J. be complaining to? But I was never asked about it because Honeybun began snitching immediately, saying the extortion plot was all Smoke's idea. This led to Honeybun's transfer to Phase 2, far from O.J., and Smoke's assignment to a new cellmate – after his release from the hole.

Cellie #3
Willy Williams
Yard name: Willy

No, the chief of police for Los Angeles during the O.J. trial did not end up becoming his third cellmate, although the somewhat lesser irony of the identical name was not lost on O.J. He had equal hatred for both of them. Willy was the only roommate O.J. would not sit with at breakfast or at church. When he walked by, O.J. would barely acknowledge him.

A chunky man in his 60s, Williams had his own

cash from a construction company he used to own before being arrested for sexual assault. So he was not impressed with O.J.'s offer to buy him into man-servitude so the home-cooked meals and folded laundry could continue. And the *last* thing Willy wanted to do is cook and clean because he already worked as a food server. (Remember, you need to work to be in O.J.'s unit.) Williams was a diet cook, ensuring that all diet orders get prepared correctly. He also loaded up and passed out the trays for dinner.

In a position like this, Willy was virtually free to bring home unused food to his cell. But he refused to do even that for O.J. He told me that he was always stolen from by his employees, which drove him crazy, so he would never take anything that wasn't his. (Willy never once received a write-up in the prison, and the culinary free staff manager speaks very highly of him.)

Not only did Williams refuse to clean up after O.J., however, he refused to clean up after himself. The guy was a total friggin' slob.

Is the *Odd Couple* theme playing in your head yet?

As many problems as Felix and Oscar had, at least they complemented one another. In prison, you can't have two Oscars. The unit officer spoke to both of them many times about the deplorable state of their cell. Remnants of dinners from days ago would become furnishings, and it smelled.

Willy also snored, farted and went to the bathroom four or five times a night, waking up O.J. every time he flushed.

"Really, Willy," O.J. would tell him, "why don't you ask the doctor for a diaper?"

What a cut-up that O.J. is. (Oops, maybe I should phrase that differently.)

CHAPTER 8:
THE GUARDS MUST BE CRAZY

Most of the guards I came across at Lovelock were intelligent, sane, decent people. But you don't want to read about them so I'll tell you all about the screw-ups.

To be fair, let me set this up a little. I grew up in Las Vegas, which is the big city to most of my co-workers. They grew up in rural Nevada, where it's like 1896 with iPhones. People think that towns where prostitution is legal must be fairly progressive. But in reality, they tolerate the brothels because their houses are all a mile apart and the only way to get a tourist to visit Main Street is to suck his dick for $500. (Also, the fact that brothels are only legal in counties with fewer than 400,000 residents may have something to do with it, too.)

You see, legal brothels may exist in rural Nevada towns like Gerlach (population 200), Mina (population 155) and Virginia City (population 855). But not a lot of black people do. And when you grow up watching gangsta rappers on MTV and then the first African-Americans you meet are the convicts who make up nearly half of the population of the prison you work for, then your stereotypes don't exactly get challenged.

At Lovelock, it wasn't only some of the prisoners who were neo-Nazis, but also some of the guards. Before O.J. arrived, they belonged to a club called the NPO (New Prison Order). In groups of five, they stormed the housing units yelling "Sieg Heil!" and throwing the Nazi salute. They would check black prisoners relentlessly and disrespect them and their property while doing so, calling them "boy" and the n-word. This was not officially allowed, but most of the members were on graveyard shift under the watch of a bad lieutenant sympathetic to their racism. This went on for months until the lieutenant brought a black inmate up for interrogation. He was handcuffed upside-down on a chair being yelled at for nothing while I just happened to walk by.

I did what any real man would do in this situation: I hid in the bathroom and cowered until I felt the coast was clear enough to sneak home. Hey, I had a new baby boy and I wanted him to have a father he could count on to remain both employed and alive. My fears were at least partially justified, since I got a threatening call the next day from the lieutenant asking me if I "thought" I saw something. He explained to me that he was in line to be the next associate warden and, if I reported anything, my career would be over.

I didn't report the situation myself, but I went to the abused inmate and gave him the name and phone number of the person he needed to report the incident to. As soon as the investigation began, one of the neo-Nazi officers rolled on everyone. Lieutenant Hitler was forced to retire and the New Prison Order was suddenly old news.

Of all the guards I would label excessively violent, I would have to give the cake to one named Camara. I don't know, but if an inmate refused to comply with an order to return a handball, I probably wouldn't have shot four rounds into him with a 12-gauge shotgun. But that's just me, I'm old-school.

When the other guards arrived on the scene, the prisoner was on the ground, bleeding and screaming, and Camara was shouting: "I told you son of a bitch if you don't give me that handball, I was going to blast you to kingdom come!"

Camara only got a letter of reprimand for what he did. But the even-sicker thing was that he became the idol of nearly every other hard-ass prison guard who has ever wanted to unload into an inmate without fear of repercussion. And there were a lot more of these guys than I thought because, for a short while, this crazy mofo ran our prison.

The reason it was only for a short while is because karma, apparently, works. While driving somewhere, Camara and his wife got into an argument. She ordered him out of the car and he complied. When Camara knocked on the car window to ask to come back in, his wife shot him twice in the heart, killing him instantly. She's now doing 25 years in a Las Vegas women's prison. (I never found out what the argument was about, but I like to think he was in possession of handball he refused to give back to her.)

There was also no shortage of the good old-fashioned kind of crazy at Lovelock. One of my esteemed colleagues, an officer with 17 years' experience, was thoroughly convinced that carbonated drinks should be banned because inmates could escape by taping multiple sodas to their belt and rocketing over the fences to freedom. This guard once showed me a three-page proposal he presented to the warden regarding this dire risk. He also accused O.J. of unauthorized time-traveling. The future, according to his theory, is where O.J. obtained the best supplements and training, which he brought back with him to the past to help young O.J. get the edge he needed to be a star at USC and in the pros. (My colleague confronted O.J. with these undeniable facts whenever O.J. wasn't paying attention and their paths crossed.)

By the way, it might surprise you how well me and this guy got along. But I always tried to keep the wackadoodles with gun access on friendly terms. "Your boy is really starting to freak me out with this time-travel shit," the Juice confided in me when he couldn't take any more.

I advised him to give in and admit the truth to the guard, that he *is* a time-traveler, then to BS him about the future. A few days later, O.J. told me he regaled the guard with the story of Earth nearly destroyed by a huge asteroid that covered it in a cloud of fire, dust and debris. The guard put his head down and walked away. Then he never talked about time travel again.

I would be remiss not to include in this chapter on guard craziness the goings-on surrounding one of the sally-port officers who checked vehicles in and out of the prison. This particular officer, who frequently cornered the Juice for strange and involuntary 20-minute conversations, once proudly told me that he did nasty things to livestock on the dairy farm where he was raised.

"TMI," I told him. But that was only the beginning of the TMI with this guy. Once, I walked into O.J.'s cell and caught this guy sniffing his mattress and pillow. When I startled him, the officer replied that he was sniffing for possible drugs. But these were deep, pleasurable sniffs. Not unless drugs get you horny do you sniff for them in this manner.

The next uncomfortable discovery about the sally-port officer I made while talking to a Nevada Highway Patrolman who visited the prison to get his uniform dry-cleaned. The state trooper asked me if I knew the sally-port officer, and how well. It turns out that the trooper once pulled him over for speeding from Lovelock to a larger Nevada town called Winnemucca. When he walked over to his car, he found him wearing a dress and makeup.

Hey, however you want to speed from Lovelock to Winnemucca is your business. But this officer was a big, ugly inbred-looking guy and that was just not an image I really needed permanently tattooed in my brain, OK? Man, I'm thinking about it now again. Can we just move onto the next chapter please?

CHAPTER 9:
THE JUICE'S HEALTH

The cane was a tough one for O.J. to accept. When he was first issued one early last year, he hid it from everyone. After a few months, the pain in his knees and left hip refused to let him.

The osteo-arthritis is due to decades of football injuries, complicated by two knee replacements, and it really slows him down. I noticed a steady decline in his speed as we walked the yard track over the years, joined by a limp beginning in 2014.

O.J. blames his arthritis for ballooning to nearly 350 pounds several times during his incarceration. If you've seen a photo of Big O.J. from the past seven years and thought, "Wow," believe me, in person, it's even more shocking. O.J. says the arthritis prevents him from exercising properly. (Of course, O.J. never blamed the burritos, nachos, lasagna and fried chicken he eats instead of salad and vegetables. Nor did I ever see him once pass on cookies or cake. This has actually led to an unofficial second yard name — one used only behind his back by a select few wiseasses: "Bobble Head.")

But the arthritis is very real, very painful and not his own fault. O.J. told me several times he thinks it will put him in a wheelchair. Yet prison officials won't let any inmate leave to treat a medical problem, like arthritis, that isn't life-threatening. The thinking is that taxpayers shouldn't foot the bill for an expensive operation – not to mention an expensive transportation operation – for conditions that can be managed with pain pills or other treatment options.

And this is where O.J.'s VIP status officially ends. Because how many more times expensive and risky would an outing like this be for the most famous American inmate in history after Al Capone? The negative publicity the prison would receive even for allowing a visit from O.J.'s private doctor is unfathomable.

Still, that doesn't mean I think O.J. is wrong to complain about the quality of medical care at Lovelock. Some of the doctors in prison are skilled practitioners who volunteer their time. But the overwhelming majority are dangerous quacks who lost the right to practice medicine on the outside. I was with O.J. when he introduced himself to the first in an undistinguished line of practitioners that would care for him over the years. O.J. reported that his arthritis was getting worse and that he needed a more powerful NSAID medication than the one he had been taking.

The doc — a gynecologist on the street — took O.J.'s vitals, checked him over and then dismissed him with the same instructions he gives all inmates who aren't suffering heart attacks in his office right that very second: "You're in perfect health, drink a lot of water."

"Are you kidding me?" O.J. asked as I walked him back to his cell. "Where the hell am I? Is Nevada serious? All this for trying to get back my sports memorabilia?"

I've only see O.J. inconsolably depressed once, and that's when his younger sister, Carmelita, died in April 2009. O.J. knew he would be granted the funeral pass to travel to California, but also that the paperwork would take two or three weeks, which meant he would miss the opportunity to pay his respects.

For the next three months, he was as miserable as inmates I witnessed who would later kill themselves. I wanted to tell him to see the prison shrink, but I couldn't. And that's because the prison shrink was batshit crazy.

This guy taught a class to the sex offenders called Stop Group. He employed drastic measures to teach them how to say no to their urges. These included spraying them in the face with a squirt gun full of water and Listerine when they gave wrong answers. He also lit matches and applied them to the backs of inmates' hands. This went on for years until the hair on one of the inmates' hands caught fire and management finally realized they had to put a stop to it. While the fired psychologist stormed out of the prison, he yelled: "You are doomed without me!"

At least O.J. got some sound advice from our dentist. The Juice spoke to him a lot. Of course, it wasn't his teeth that were ever the topic of conversation, but sports betting. Later, I found out that this dentist used to also be a bookie, which is what led to the removal of his dental license. He eventually lost his job at Lovelock for soliciting prostitution.

CHAPTER 10:
FINDING JESUS, TRADING HIM FOR MUHAMMAD AND A PLAYER TO BE NAMED LATER

After his first year inside, I noticed O.J. attending more services at the prison chapel, a room inside Operations that seats 50 inmates. At first, it was Sundays and then it was also Wednesdays. He began talking about church on the yard with other inmates. Then a Bible appeared next to his bed. He explained that religion was good because he needed to keep his head up and being a religious person in the prison will do that.

Church also reminded O.J. of his mother, Eunice Simpson, a lifelong member of the Evergreen Baptist Church, a lifelong volunteer for the Salvation Army and, late in life, a teacher of Bible classes at a senior center. O.J. loved her very much. Wanting to see her was the reason he gave police for ending the Bronco chase back at his mansion in Brentwood. (He didn't realize that she had been hospitalized for heart palpitations caused by the situation.)

Religion gave Eunice the strength to endure her son's tribulations. (She lived until 2001.) And O.J. was convinced it could do the same for him.

But in 2013, O.J.'s appeal for a re-trial was denied and his spirit crushed. Faced with four or more years in the slammer, he decided to try something different — something suggested to him on the outside by fellow former fallen athlete Mike Tyson.

The Elders of Islam, the official Lovelock Muslim prisoners organization, couldn't have been more overjoyed by O.J.'s decision to convert. As public-relations coups go, it was like the Beatles going with the Maharashi to India. They got him a traditional Kufi prayer cap and a prayer rug for his prison cell. But O.J. wasn't ready to turn his back on Jesus after getting to know him so well for the previous five years. So a period of intense confusion ensued, as the Koran joined the Bible by O.J.'s bedside.

The Christians didn't seem to mind O.J. going Muslim, as long as he still reported to church. But the Muslims told O.J. he needed to choose a master. They applied increasing pressure on him to convert. They walked the track with him. They even approached me and asked if I could talk him into it because of how much better off O.J. would be as a Muslim.

Some of O.J.'s Christian friends were not very Christian when he finally decided to trade Jesus in for Muhammed. They were very freaking angry, in fact, after O.J. took his Bible back to the Christian inmate shot-caller. And so it was that a holy war broke out inside Lovelock....

O.J. was kicked out of one of his fantasy football leagues and fired from the softball team he had been coaching for three years, the White Sox, which was composed entirely of Christians. So O.J. formed a new team from scratch, the Cardinals, consisting entirely of — woah, what do you know? — Muslims. They went on to beat the White Sox in the most intense championship softball game I have ever witnessed, by the way. (It ended in pushing and shoving and, for the first time in Lovelock history, winning and losing teams who refused to shake hands.)

The Muslims couldn't be happier, of course. Recruitment to Islam in the prison skyrocketed and outside volunteers lined up to facilitate in prayer rituals.

There was one thing O.J. loved more than Allah, however, and that was sweets. Ramadan, the fourth of five pillars of Islam, requires all Muslims to fast between dawn and sunset each day for a month, and the Juice just couldn't do it. (Unlike Lovelock, the Muslims refused to write any O.J exceptions into their rule book.)

The Elders placed somebody on O.J. as much as they could, trying to keep his mind and mouth off food, but eventually, the time came each day when they had to leave O.J. to his own devices. And these devices usually included cookies and cake.

If there were a religion that worshiped cookies and cake, O.J. could be its most devoted disciple. That man loved cookies so much, he almost let them ruin his parole....

In 2013, a culinary worker stole a batch of oatmeal cookies from work that he and a dozen other inmates inhaled on the Unit 6A tier. O.J. knew this was illegal and that he would be singled out if caught, but he just couldn't help himself. Naturally, when the cookie gang was caught, the night-shift officer did single O.J. out. While she didn't follow through on her threat to write him up for possessing contraband, a witness leaked the embarrassing story to the *National Enquirer* and it made world headlines.

After he violated Ramadan for a week straight, O.J. came to me for some Jew-Juice time advice. "Should I be honest with them about cheating, Felix?" he asked.

I'm a Jew. What the hell do I know about Ramadan? But I do enjoy a good opportunity to bullshit. So I told O.J. that it was not a Ramadan violation to eat snacks *accidentally*. (Fittingly, O.J. replied that I sounded like Robert Shapiro.)

My advice was ignored and an O.J. confession promptly issued to the elders. Not wanting to lose their star recruitment tool, they gave him what any 10-year-old boy will recognize as a do-over.

"Make up the Ramadan at a later date," they said.

This was the point, I believe, at which O.J. lost faith in Islam. He began to question whether the only reason the elders wanted him was for his fame. Second, and more importantly, he knew he could never accomplish a fast, however long it was put off for his sake.

"My heart just isn't as strong as my appetite," he told me.

Within a week, the Bible was back.

Praise be, cookies and cake!

CHAPTER 11:
THE REAL NAKED GUN — O.J.'S PENIS

One of the most common questions I've been asked by friends and radio-show hosts since announcing this book is the size of Juice's johnson. Men and women both want to know.

"Does he clang his penis along the bars of his cell when he needs something?" someone asked me on Facebook.

At first, I refused to respond. This is information I obtained while in a position of complete authority over another human being. If the inmate I was guarding was female and I reported on what she looked like in her birthday suit, the world would hate me almost as much as it does O.J.

But I didn't invent our male-dominated society, I just live in it. Besides, O.J. was proud of his endowment and made no attempt to cover up the one time I was in his unit while he was returning from the shower. Of course, that didn't mean he consented to a report on his penis filling an entire chapter of a book.

So I have decided to compromise and handle O.J.'s penis delicately.

Did you enjoy that joke I just made there? Well, then you would love living in a men's prison. For the straight guys — inmates and workers — playful homophobic references are a favorite way to relieve the tension. (One of O.J.'s favorite things to say is "I love you" followed by "but not in a sexual way.")

Anyway, back to O.J.'s dick dangling right there in front of me....

I asked whether being naked around other guys was something O.J. enjoyed. (See: homophobic references, above.)

"OK, Felix," he responded. "My garden hose and I are going back to my cell to get a nap before dinner."

All I will say is that this was not *that much* of an exaggeration.

O.J.'s huge penis is the stuff of Lovelock legend. One of the female officers (out of 160 guards, 20 are female) even enjoyed conducting her own ongoing investigation while on shower duty. O.J. noticed that, a minute after she saw him walk in, she would suddenly be wearing prescription glasses.

This wasn't a fluke. It occurred every time he took his late-afternoon shower and she was there. No glasses and then – blam! — glasses. And she'd be staring more at his stall more than the others.

"This unit officer is *shower-sharking* me," O.J. told me.

It was a compliment and a rare change of pace from being ogled by people of the same sex. Nevertheless, O.J. felt violated. So he asked if he should report it. No, I told him, since he would be the obvious rat, which could lead to retaliation.

Instead, O.J. owned the situation. The next day, he told me, he stopped by the officer and instructed her: "You should put your glasses on, shower shark, I am headed to the shower."

"What are you talking about, Mr. Simpson?" she asked.

"Is that right?" O.J. replied. (That's one of his favorite phrases. He uses it to great comedic effect to defuse tense situations.)

The education officer also had a huge crush. She would always invite O.J. into her office for lunch. She also started wearing tons of makeup and perfume. The Juice told me she asked him what his favorite perfume was. She also asked whether he would consider dating her upon his release from prison. (O.J. told me he always acted like he didn't hear the question.) She was an otherwise very sweet person, so neither O.J. nor me considered reporting her.

One of the inmates who claimed to have more than a shower-room familiarity with O.J.'s penis was a former transsexual prostitute named Jazmena Jameson. By far the closest facsimile to a female we had among the inmates, Jameson worked as porter in laundry, which gave her access to O.J.'s boxers. (Nope, not briefs. Should I have made that its own chapter? God, sometimes I hate myself for writing this book.)

So anyway, how did Jameson know the boxers were O.J.'s? Because inmates write their names in them. No one, gay or straight, wants another guy's racing stripes riding up their ass but their own. For 99.9999 percent of all inmates in the history of history, this system poses no problems.

If you're O.J. Simpson, however, then the former transsexual prostitute working in laundry will hold your boxers hostage and try to get you to visit her cell to retrieve them.

"If you want your boxers back," O.J. was told through an intermediary, "you have to let Jazmena give you oral sex."

O.J. had no problem being admired by other inmates or even being hit on. Gay guys would constantly ask to clean his cell, make food for him, anything he needed. O.J. was, for many, the ultimate conquest, and he accepted that as the fact it was.

So he laughed off Jameson's overtures and kissed his boxers goodbye.

Then Jameson's story suddenly changed from "I want to give O.J. head" to "I gave O.J. head." And that unnerved O.J., who worried that the mainstream media would get wind of the story and believe it without investigating. He appealed to his favorite prison guard to intervene.

When I paid Jameson a visit and asked her to knock it off, she broke down. She told me of her secret plan to extract O.J.'s DNA from his underwear to help sell a bogus story about her affair with O.J. to the *National Enquirer*. She had no money and was desperate, and they were offering five figures. When Jameson learned that her plan wouldn't work, she tried her luck seeking an actual mouth full of Simpson semen.

Granted, DNA evidence isn't usually much of an obstacle for O.J. Simpson. But in the court of public opinion, you don't get to hire a Johnny Cochran.

More importantly, a story like this would have been bad for the prison. So I cashed in a favor and got Jameson transferred to another prison detail. She sold the story anyway, without any evidence to back it up. It ran in 2014 under the headline "O.J. Simpson's Transexual Lover Tells All: 'We Had Sex & I'm HIV Positive.'"

"I ended up having oral sex with him," Jameson claimed in a videotaped "confession." "I walked up on him and said, 'You can stop me if you want to,' but I knew he wasn't gonna stop me."

I hope you enjoyed my chapter about O.J. Simpson's penis. Are you proud of me, mom, or what?

CHAPTER 12:
KARDASHIANS KEEPING UP
WITH O.J.

The Juice has several rivals for the title of most hated celebrity in America, and quite a few of them share the last name Kardashian. That's ridiculous, since being annoying is hardly a capital crime. But, as I have personally witnessed, O.J. and the Kardashians are connected on many other levels, some of which are bizarre.

While you probably remember that Robert Kardashian was the Armenian-American attorney who sat by O.J.'s side throughout the first criminal murder trial, you might not know why. Kardashian wasn't just the attorney O.J. hired to defend him. (In fact, he wasn't even an attorney, since he let his license lapse before the trial.) Robert was the best friend that O.J. demanded a permanent seat for on his "Dream Team."

When Robert picked Kris Jenner up from the airport for their first date, O.J. was in the car with them. O.J. and Nicole double-dated with Robert and Kris constantly, even after the Kardashian kids came along. (They referred to them as "Auntie Nicole and Uncle O.J.") And a bizarre video that Kris taped for her own 30th birthday, in 1985, featured O.J. and other friends singing "She loves you!" as part of the rewritten lyrics to Randy Newman's "I Love L.A." (Search for it on YouTube.)

It was to Robert's house that O.J. ran when the warrant was issued for his arrest in 1994. O.J. locked himself in Khloe's room, threatening to kill himself right there. (If it happened, Kim might not have even needed a sex tape to launch her family's career in fame, or whatever it is that they do.)

The Simpson and Kardashian couples were so tight, it has led some to speculate that they may have mixed and matched in other combinations. And, after about a year of nonstop tabloid speculation that O.J. was more to Khloe than just a pretend uncle, I decided to exploit my unprecedented access and ask. What the hey, it was more interesting than what they were serving in the canteen that day.

O.J. replied that, no, he was not Khloe's biological father. He and Bob were best friends, he told me, so he would never "tap" Kris.

You can sort of tell when the Juice believes a story he's telling you — or at least when he's rehearsed believing it enough times — because he'll look you straight in the eye, unflinching, while telling it. One thing I'll always remember about the way O.J. answered that question is how he glanced downward while doing so.

Personally, I think the affair may have happened, but that, if so, O.J. deeply regrets it and cares too much about Khloe — who was born a year before Kris' birthday video — to risk causing her any further pain by revealing it.

If the affair did happen, my guess is that even O.J. doesn't know for sure whether it resulted in Khloe's conception, and that he probably doesn't want to know. This is consistent with how he answered when I asked if he'd be willing to take a paternity test: "no." It also explains why O.J. told me that Khloe has asked many times over the years for him to explain to the media that she is not his daughter, and that he has refused every time. (They would probably demand a paternity test.)

Even after the Kardashians divorced in 1991 and Kris married Bruce Jenner one month later, a new Simpson-Kardashian foursome formed because O.J. was already tight with the Olympic champion.

The relationship between the Juice and Bruce Jenner began shortly after Jenner – a perfect specimen of muscular manhood at 26 years old, 6'2" and 194 lbs. – won the decathlon, the most difficult Olympic sport, in 1976. He was the world's most famous athlete, but had no money to show for it. So he approached O.J. to ask how one goes about converting one's sports notoriety into cash via endorsements — like O.J.'s for Hertz.

The Juice hooked him up with his manager, then began golfing and running in the same social circles as Jenner. (What young Los Angeles female could resist a play from not one but two of the most desirable athletes on the planet?)

Other than cheating on Kris four times while they were married, O.J. told me, Jenner is an otherwise great person. (That kind of behavior apparently doesn't bother O.J., if you catch my drift.)

But the O.J. murder case drove a knife through the Kardashian/Simpson friendship. And that's because Nicole was Kris' best friend. (Kendall Jenner, who was born shortly after the murders, was given the middle name Nicole in her memory.) In her memoir, Kris wrote that Nicole told her numerous times: "He's going to kill me, and he's going to get away with it." Kris claims Nicole was convinced that someone – either O.J. or someone sent by him — was looking through her windows and climbing through her bushes in the middle of the night.

On the day O.J. was to be arrested for the murders, it was Robert he turned to first. In fact, Robert told Barbara Walters that the former gridiron legend locked himself "in his daughter's bedroom" with a gun pointed to his head. (Kardashian never specified which daughter, since none were famous yet.)

Kris split with her former husband a second time over the murder case, and hasn't spoken to O.J. since 1995, when he called her from jail proclaiming his innocence. But I can attest to some Kardashian/Simpson contact continuing over the years, apparently behind Kris' back. Up to five times a week, on one of the unit's four payphones, O.J. regularly caught up with Kim Kardashian and her rapper husband, Kanye West, talking football and vacations and never once debating the details of his complete innocence of every crime he was ever charged with. (Other frequent O.J. phone calls were placed to Al Cowlings, obviously, and to San Francisco 49ers tight end Vernon Davis, who either lives with the Juice's nephew or hangs out there quite a lot.)

It was during one of O.J.'s frequent conversations with Khloe Kardashian late in 2014 that he told me he received the first heads up that someone in the family was acting "very strangely."

Bruce Jenner's gender transition took the kids in the family by surprise. It shocked them silly, according to O.J. And, just as shockingly, it was O.J. who provided the voice of sanity to help them deal with their emotions.

O.J. immediately accepted Bruce's journey into Caitlyn. "Whatever makes him happy," he told me, smiling and shrugging. In fact, when the *Vanity Fair* story broke, O.J. cut out Caitlyn's cover photo and taped it on his shirt, over his heart, proudly wearing it to the gym. (It was this action that probably resulted in a *National Enquirer* story claiming that O.J. has professed having the "hots" for Caitlyn. Seriously?)

I think O.J. saw supporting Caitlyn as a way to atone for his rejection of his father. I don't even think it was subconscious. To someone who cut his own father out of his life for being involuntarily different, I'm positive he felt that helping a friend through gender reassignment would have a healing effect.

Unfortunately for O.J., Caitlyn didn't want that support. O.J. told me one of the Kardashians (either Khloe or Kim) told him she heard Caitlyn call O.J. "a murderer who deserved to be in prison for the rest of his miserable life."

Immediately, O.J. ripped up the photo of Caitlyn and complained that Bruce wouldn't even be a celebrity without his help — not an unreasonable argument since gymnast Nadia Comaneci was a huge star at the same Olympics, yet failed to find a hook in pop culture and is now a Trivial Pursuit answer.

CHAPTER 13:
O.J. ON THE MURDERS

The thing it was tough to wrap my brain around at first when O.J. discussed Nicole is that it's possible to feel pain over a loved one's murder that's genuine, *even if you're the one who's responsible*. Of course, I'm not arguing that O.J.'s thinly veiled regret deserves any sympathy. He *should* feel pain for what he did to those two poor people, and much, much more. But it was fascinating for me to watch O.J. choke up whenever he discussed the woman to whom he kept a shrine at the head of his bunk. He said their time together was the best time of his life, and that she was the one woman to whom he remained faithful.

I believe that 100 percent — at least the first part. You don't nearly sever the head off someone you feel less than passionately about. But Nicole was very strong-willed. She was the one thing he couldn't control — until he finally figured out a way.

Nicole was just 19 when O.J. hit her for the first time. This I didn't learn from O.J. but from the Internet. Being the Juice's BFF means you have to constantly hit the Internet if you want to know what time it really is. The next day after being hit for the first time, according to the Internet and not the Juice, she found a new Porsche in the driveway for her. O.J. thought that his fame and riches meant he could get away with anything. For a long time, he was right.

Every anniversary, O.J. told me more than once, he and Nicole would drink really expensive champagne and eat calamari together. While having sex with every other conquest after Nicole, he continued, he still thought about her.

You have no idea how many times I was dying to interrupt O.J. and say: "Well, if you loved her so much, then maybe you shouldn't have killed her." But I was always curious to hear more, never to cut it off, to see where he might take it. It was like a reality show shot and screened just for me.

Watching that TV special marking the 20th anniversary of the murders with O.J. felt like communing directly with my younger self. Like I was closing a circle or something. And let me tell you, when I told my younger self what was happening, he thought I was full of shit. I was watching those same images I remember from back on that TV above the bar at the Cheyenne Saloon, only the action featured a play-by-play by the only guy who knew what he was thinking at the time.

"That's the thing, I *didn't* know," O.J. told me. "I wanted to kill myself. I lost everything, and now I was going to jail?"

I noticed how it was all about what had happened *to him*. Nicole's death was something that happened *to him*. O.J. Simpson's wife was killed. How dare someone? She was a trophy to him, just like the one at the Palace Station that landed him in my life.

As we watched the Bronco lead cops to O.J.'s Brentwood estate live in front of hundreds of millions of people, he continued talking. I didn't say a word.

"I opened my mouth and stuck a loaded gun in," he said. "Bob had to talk me out of it. Sometimes, I wish he didn't."

Look, O.J. has made it clear that he agrees with the State of California's legal finding of his innocence. So you don't get to remain a confidante by asking, "Hey O.J., be honest, did you kill Nicole and Ron?" (By the way, O.J. insists that *If I Did It: Confessions of the Killer,* the 2007 book purported to contain his "hypothetical description" of the murders, was not written by him; that he was paid only not to dispute it. And this is one O.J. story it's not difficult for me to believe. I've seen O.J.'s notes and holy crap. I mean, I thought I had trouble with spelling and grammar — props to my co-writer, Corey Levitan! — but those O.J. notes made me feel like an English teacher.)

The closest I ever came to confronting O.J. was a joke that he didn't find funny at all. It was during a segment of the 20th anniversary special that laid out scenarios about who killed Nicole and Ron if O.J. didn't.

I asked O.J. to come over to his sink to look at something. He complied and was staring into his mirror when I told him he just solved the murders. He gave me a dirty look. At first, he thought I was just busting his balls. But I returned his dirty look and, for a couple of seconds, he glimpsed the real me.

The staff barber, an inmate in for murder, claims he was able to get O.J. to confess by tricking him when they first met. According to his story, he introduced himself as Randy, Ronald Goldman's brother. He claims he told O.J. he was in for murder and then got a confession, murderer-to-murderer.

Randy's story always struck me as BS because if Ronald had a brother named Randy, you figure O.J. would have known that. If Ronald had a brother named Randy who was arrested for murder, O.J. *definitely* would have known that. But it's the kind of story I imagine lots of inmates spread among themselves. When you're locked up and forgotten by the outside world, the need to feel significant in any way becomes more important than the need to remain honest. That's why the tabloids are full of O.J. information from inmates who completely made it up.

There was one Jew-Juice time that nearly resulted in a confession, however. It was on one of what would have been O.J. and Nicole's wedding anniversaries. He went into his usual story about drinking champagne and eating calamari, forgetting that he had already told me several times. And so I asked. I didn't confront, I asked: "Do you have anything you'd like to get off your chest about the murders?"

He shared with me a cryptic statement that he later pretended never slipped out: "Only two people alive know the truth: me and Al Cowlings." Then he immediately changed the subject to the softball team he coached.

Now I'm no criminal scientist, but there is no possible way another individual can *know* you're innocent of a crime unless he happened to have been with you while you weren't committing said crime. And no one has ever placed Cowlings with Simpson at the time of the murders, doing something else.

The theory O.J. shared with me and other prisoners was that Nicole and Ron ran up a $30k cocaine debt with their dealer, who came to O.J.'s Brentwood house with one of his buddies to demand payment. When O.J. refused, they said they were headed to Goldman's to scare him into either paying up or dealing drugs for them out of the restaurant.

This happens to conflict with the argument his defense made during the trial. They claimed one or more hit men were hired by the drug dealers to look for Brown's friend, Faye Resnick, a known cocaine user who failed to pay her drug bill and who entered rehab four days before the killings, after staying at Nicole's condo for several days. When they found Brown and Goldman instead, they both received "Colombian necklaces." (Judge Ito barred testimony about Resnick's drug use, calling the proposed motive "highly speculative.")

Shortly before my retirement, O.J. broached an admission for a second time. He didn't say *the words*, only that he "wishes he could do it all again and change things." His hands were shaking and his eyes watering as he confided in me how much he missed Nicole and his friendship with Kris Kardashian.

"Would you still look at me the same way if I did something in my lifetime that was horrible, Felix?"

he asked me.

I told him that yes, I would. And that wasn't a lie, because I never thought he didn't kill Ron and Nicole.

That was as close as I was going to get.

CHAPTER 14:
A JUICY GOODBYE

On September 21, 2015, I was released from prison. In a way, it felt like that. Prison institutionalizes everyone within its walls to some degree — even those who get to go home at night. You think harder, trust people less, and learn to rely on others instead of your own gut. For an illness, I walk to the infirmary. I have no "internal medicine specialist." If I get hungry, I walk to culinary. For a haircut, I walk to the prison barber.

It will take me a long time to correct that thinking – if I ever can.

Our last Jew-Juice time saw O.J. and me sitting on a bench outside his unit, staring at the brown mountains. They said it reminded him of the location where he shot the movie *Capricorn One*. He said he got "more pussy" during that shoot than he ever dreamed he'd get in his whole life.

O.J. and I talked about the importance of being a good dad to my boys, who were 14 and 17 at the time. He told me he was proud of my boys for wanting to become nurses and not following the typical male stereotype.

"My mom was a nurse," he said. "When you dedicate your life to helping people, it makes you a better person. It means you're probably a better person to start with."

O.J. will probably follow me out the gates in 2017, since he was already granted parole on five of the criminal counts he was sentenced for. He told me he plans to move in with his oldest daughter, 47-year-old Arnelle, who owns two townhouses in Florida. He'll stay there for as long as it takes until he gets back on his feet.

O.J. will never have to work again. He told me he'll have roughly $11k a month coming in from his retirement funds — the NFL, Social Security, the Screen Actor's Guild and a TV pension.

He told me he wants to live a drama-free existence — no sports-memorabilia raids! — but worries whether he'll be able to afford the 24/7 security team necessary to keep the TMZ cameras and assorted dangerous kooks at bay.

"Hey, you wanna be on my security team?" he asked.

O.J. said he was happy for me but sad for himself. He said he will think of me every time he goes to the gym, since that's where we met. But he said it wouldn't be long before his release, and he can't wait to grab a mojito with me on the outside.

O.J. thanked me for my friendship, and I thanked him for teaching me a few things I didn't realize about myself. It's true, though. I became a better father and son thanks to a double-murderer.

After about 40 minutes, O.J. stood up and hugged me. He asked me to please not repeat any of our conversations to anyone.

I'm not holding my breath for that mojito.

POST-SCRIPT:
McDONALD'S CLUB ACCESS!

My dad finally invited me to his McDonald's Club. It was after a heart-to-heart phone call I forced him to have about all the feelings that writing this book brought up.

He told me I was right — that he expected his son to do better than him and it disappointed him that I didn't. He realized he was wrong not to let that go long ago.

I arrived at the McDonald's on Eastern Ave. and Russell Road at 7:15 am and saw a group of five men in the back. I immediately recognized the Detroit cop and the UNLV professor, and I correctly picked the oldest guy out as the WWII vet.

"This is my favorite son," Dad said. (Of course, I'm his only, so there's that.)

I introduced myself to everyone, correctly guessing most of their names. My dad also introduced me to a McDonald's security guard he knew who walked over.

They told me that my father always brags about the TVs and other gifts I buy for him.

"Isn't that what a son is supposed to do for his father?" I asked.

Later, Dad told me he was glad we had our chat and that I am the greatest son ever. He told me he loved me for the first time. And, also for the first time, I told him.

Now that I'm a published author, however, of course my father's going to be proud of me. So does any of this really count?

Just kidding. It totally counts.

CPSIA information can be obtained
at www.ICGtesting.com
Printed in the USA
BVOW03s1145170817
491735BV00036B/2/P